Breakthrough
for a broken heart

*Overcome Your Disappointments
and Blossom Into Your Dreams!*

Paul Davis

**CREATION
HOUSE**
A STRANG COMPANY

Breakthrough for a Broken Heart
by Paul Davis
Published by Creation House
A Strang Company
600 Rinehart Road
Lake Mary, Florida 32746
www.creationhouse.com

All Scripture quotations are from the New King James Version of the Bible. Copyright © 1979, 1980, 1982 by Thomas Nelson Inc. Used by permission.

Special thanks to Dr. Mark Chironna for being a continual source of inspiration and revelation. Your teachings have lifted me to the heights of heaven and strengthened my soul.

Cover design by Mark Labbe

Library of Congress Control Number: 2005939107
International Standard Book Number: 1-59979-003-3

First Edition

06 07 08 09 10 — 9 8 7 6 5 4 3 2 1
Printed in the United States of America

Contents

Introduction

*H*AVE YOU EVER been disappointed in a relationship, or in your professional life? Have you ever acted in desperation to save a relationship? Why do we, when seeking love, often drive away the ones we desire the most? What can be done to correct such behavior? Does love seem to continually elude your grasp? Have past relational hurts affected your relationship possibilities? Have you ever experienced a personal ground zero? If any of these situations sound familiar, then this book will help you to recover and bounce back. We will address such questions and probe the depths of both the human heart and the psyche to get to the root of such issues that affect us both relationally and professionally.

Life's challenges and the emotional complexities that unexpectedly come with it are not so easy to bear at times. Within one year I experienced the loss of my beloved grandmother, a devastating divorce, identity theft, and a hurricane that destroyed my house. The emotional ride can be a roller coaster—full of ups and downs. Only this ride is not something we necessarily stand in line for and pay to participate in. Nevertheless it makes passengers of us all at some point in our lives, and thereby enables us to empathize with others who are suffering in similar situations.

Over two years ago now (at the writing of this book), after returning from a month of ministering in Africa, I got an earful concerning my wife's infidelity on the way home from the airport. Upon hearing this grievous news I was speechless. I was overwhelmed and cut to the core. It was as if I was dead within, numbed by the betrayal. When she remained unrepentant and continued her wayward path, I had to pull the plug. Upon getting myself together, I served her with divorce papers. That was after two months in which I made every effort to reconcile. Yet my attempts proved futile as the callous heart of my spouse did not respond to three weeks of flowers, breakfast in bed, and cards.

Such unconditional and self-effacing love left me feeling very vulnerable. Yet I was willing to pay the price as it was the only hope to preserve our marriage. Of the nine counseling sessions I attended, my wife appeared at one. Meanwhile I sought wisdom and insight from pastors, prophets, and anyone willing to give advice.

The breaking point came when my wife looked at me one day and commented on my relentless effort to win her back with a particularly cruel remark. From that point, I knew I had not won her back. Upon hearing her derogatory remark, I knew her state of mind and the condition of her heart.

The fighter in me arose and I began to wage a war within. The battle began as I sought to harness my emotions and focus my affections on loving me first. This warrior immediately rose to the occasion and began to initiate his endgame as the divorce proceedings drew near.

The level of self-ministry and mastery needed to bounce back from such a monumental setback and huge blow to my self-esteem required all of my focus. I made a conscious choice not to bury my desires beneath my disappointments, but to lift up my head and look forward. Upon doing so, I moved forth with bold determination that has since catapulted me to new levels in my life that I had never known before my personal ground zero. I pray that this candid portrait from my heart will heal your heart, fill you with purpose, inspire you to action, and thrust you forward into your future with a fiery zeal.

This is your finest hour. You may have been knocked down, but certainly you are not knocked out. Get up and go for it again. You may be broken—but breakthrough is on the way!

Hurt people, hurt people.

If your heart is in need, plant a love seed.

If you need love, give it away.

Lend a helping hand. Help your heart.

Those who need love the most
often deserve it the least.

ONE

Hungry Heart

EVERYONE HAS A hungry heart. All of us deeply yearn for and crave genuine love. The acceptance and affirmation that unconditional love generates for the human heart and soul is boundless. Such love is immeasurable as it fills us, makes life flow with creative juice, and quenches fear in an instant.

From childhood I hungered for love. Because my parents divorced when I was a baby, I often felt a sense of emotional inadequacy. It was like a grand canyon in my soul. Being raised by my grandparents enabled me to get much of the love I needed, though I still felt some emotional gaps within.

My mom suffered with addictions and consequently she was never around. That left me without the affection one would normally get in their early years. I never gave it much thought until the time I saw my baby brother cuddling with my stepmother one day. I suddenly recognized the true mother-son intimacy I had missed. Something awakened inside me; my heart hurt deep within, as I realized what I had never received as a child.

Thankfully my precious grandmother, whom I affectionately called Nana, was there for me throughout my formative years. Yet there can be a difference between the love a mother and a grandmother gives a child. The love of a mother seems deeper, coming from a biological origin and is more socially empowering considering there is less of an age difference. The age gap with grandparents can make the bridge to the present a longer walk. Yet that is not to diminish what a grandparent can do for a child, especially when the child does not have a parent's involvement.

I cannot imagine the depth of hurt and pain others must experience who are fully without mother or grandmother, father or grandfather. Maybe it is what I felt, but multiplied one hundredfold.

All of us desire love and the depth of personal contentment it brings. Not all of us however know how to go about getting it. This is why many resort to violence; they cannot cope or take living without love anymore. When kids are shunned and mocked by their peers, unable to find a source of love and acceptance, the schoolyard becomes a battleground. This is certainly not justifiable, but it is understandable. The deepest of all human needs is to be loved. Unfortunately many of us have not been taught how to see that our needs are met properly while remaining true to our values.

Many inwardly long and wait for someone to acknowledge and respond to them. While such longings are justifiable, they are not empowering. That is to say, if you are always waiting for a feeling, you may be waiting for a very long time.

People longing and hurting for love can often lash out in the most unusual ways. In one case, a precious widow began criticizing her grandchildren, calling them selfish, spoiled brats. Instead of serving her purpose to help her get what she ultimately wanted, it did the opposite and drove her grandkids further away from her. We do not realize that when we are hurting the most is when we are most likely to hurt the ones we love. Hurt people hurt other people.

A LOVE WORTH GIVING AWAY

Love is the deepest core value for many of us, however merely valuing something cannot bring it into your life. You must first give, and draw it near to you. This means if you have a need, plant a seed. You can experience no harvest until you have first planted, watered, and cultivated a seed. Therefore you must remove your focus from your need and direct it toward your seed. I know this is easier said than done when your heart is broken and in dire need.

A better approach is to go on the offensive, to take the initiative. This means you show love first rather than wait for someone to express love to you. Such expressions of love can be shown in numerous ways to people of all sorts, both worthy and unworthy of your love. Fulfillment comes when you change your personal rules that lead to satisfying your core values.

The person that says to herself, "I will feel love when he says this and does that for me," is sabotaging her personal happiness and setting herself up for disappointment. Such a rule is disempowering because it has nothing to do with you and everything to do with someone over whom you have no control.

Take the initiative by first rewriting your personal rules for feeling love. Write rules that empower you to feel love when you give love, be it through a smile, touch, act of kindness, or spoken word. Then you don't have to wait on anybody else, but rather the feeling of love is generated by you when you choose to.

Some examples of empowering rules for love could be:

1. I feel love rapidly and powerfully when I focus on others and concern myself with their needs.

2. I feel love immediately when I reach out with a smile, a touch, a spoken word, or an act of kindness.

3. I feel love regardless of what others do or say because I love and appreciate myself.

Understandably, we all want someone to lean on, who we can trust to be there for us. Yet sadly, not all of us have that blessing readily available to us all the time. Therefore, we must find other ways to satisfy our yearning for love. My grandfather, Pop-Pop as I affectionately called him, was known as the nicest man in the world. Everywhere he went he acknowledged and recognized people, cordially interacted with them, and made an effort to brighten up their day. It did not matter if it was a gas station attendant, food service rep, or laborer, Pop-Pop would always treat everybody with the same loving respect. Such a positive attitude and friendly disposition endeared people to him. He quickly made friends everywhere and in so doing helped his own heart along the way.

Help your heart by unconditionally loving everybody. Whether it's a lonely widow, a hospital patient, a bored child, or someone close to you, reach out to others and watch the love come surging back to you. Spread the love and soon you will reap a harvest of profound gratitude.

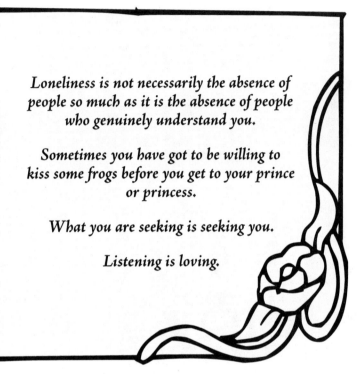

Loneliness is not necessarily the absence of people so much as it is the absence of people who genuinely understand you.

Sometimes you have got to be willing to kiss some frogs before you get to your prince or princess.

What you are seeking is seeking you.

Listening is loving.

Two

Lonely Heart

*T*HE VIDEO FOR Kelly Clarkson's song "Breakaway" shows a young girl in the presence of her mother and siblings, but she really doesn't want to be there. Far away in her own dreamland she visualizes where she wants to be. The reality however is that she is still surrounded with family who probably know nothing about her internal world, and even if they did might not fully understand.

How many of us have people in our lives who are similarly distant? If not disinterested, perhaps they are trying to put their ideological map on us and even worse, occasionally live vicariously through us to be personally fulfilled themselves. Sadly, they are often in our immediate family. It is too easy to remove ourselves from people outside our family, but how can we have nothing to do with those in our family? Well, at least it is not as easy to blow them off—is it?

As the old adage goes, "you can choose your friends, not your family." I love my family, but that is not to say they always understand me or where I am in my life's journey. Of course, we all wish for the perfect family that genuinely listens, that fully understands and affirms us. Yet the reality is that we are not always quick to listen, patient to understand, or lovingly affirm. Thankfully I am blessed with a wonderful father and mother who always take time to have heart-to-heart talks with me and eagerly listen to what I have to say.

Unfortunately for many people, their family can often be the first ones to put them under the microscope and scrutinize them. As family, I suppose some people assume they are somehow entitled to influence the course of our lives. Only family can get away with this. Anyone else who dared to try and impose their beliefs on us would not succeed.

Excluding the fact that our parents would never admit to trying to tell us what to do, their subtle statements speak for themselves as they often try to steer us. Motives can range from public image and status to what is best for the parent when they are old and need you to care for them. Most parents however just want the best for their kids and their intentions are pure, despite an occasional mixed motive or unorthodox method to pursue their own interest in the name of "what's best for you" as their child.

UNDERSTANDING AND DEVELOPING TRUST

Loneliness is not a fun condition to endure at all. After my grandfather died, my Nana lost the twinkle in her eye. There was such a depth of understanding and mutual trust between them. As I cared for my Nana in her old age, she often seemed empty inside.

I have learned that real, deep loneliness is not resolved by the presence of people. Having more people around does not necessarily alleviate loneliness. Loneliness is the absence of people who understand you. When we have just one person nearby who knows and understands us, we can feel cared for and hopeful. Friends and family such as this are invaluable. It is often not in what they say or do as much as it is in the sympathetic ear they provide that enables our soul to take rest and comfort in their presence.

Let's come up with some empowering rules for ourselves to quickly overcome loneliness. Feel free to develop your own rules:

1. When loneliness arises in me I honor it but do not sink deeper into it. I realize loneliness is simply a signal and indicator telling me I need to spread my love

among more people who also desire a sense of significance and togetherness.

2. I happily welcome loneliness because it compels me to move with courage, beyond comfort, and out into the world where hurting and lonely people exist.

3. When I feel lonely I receive it as a gift that is telling me to feel the loneliness others are experiencing. I embrace such a feeling and give myself to its magnetic pull until I reach out and brighten someone else's day who seems to be alone.

4. Since loneliness is just my Creator's way of telling me that others in the world need me, I am never alone. Instead I recognize that I am wanted. Hence the feeling of loneliness is endeavoring to bring me out of myself and take me to others to whom I am predestined and sent.

Following my divorce I met a special young lady over a single's Web site with whom I found a deep connection. The first time we spoke over the telephone we talked for seven hours. Though she lived on the other side of the country, the immediate connection was so profound and stimulating that I gladly endured the time difference to talk to her every night. I often went to bed in the early morning hours after talking to her. Yet it was a small sacrifice to talk to someone for whom I had an affinity.

Sometimes you have to be willing to kiss some frogs before you get to your prince or princess. This is what often disheartens many and causes them to stop the search altogether. Life however is a marathon, not a sprint. You must think for the long term and not throw in the towel so easily. There is certainly someone out there for you.

As a dear friend repeatedly told me, "What you are seeking is seeking you." If you have a desire, a longing unfulfilled, then there must be someone capable of satisfying that yearning. God is not unjust to give you a desire without creating someone capable of fulfilling that yearning. Just don't give up!

I was amazed to meet a lovely lady who lived in Paris and was deeply committed to remaining pure unto God and her future husband. Though she was very beautiful and growing impatient to marry, this outstanding woman was intent on waiting for the right man rather than selling out and short-changing herself.

Though we did not feel meant for each other, we did have some great times together as friends. I took her to see *Phantom of the Opera* and she took me around Paris.

Be resilient. Be incessant. Let go of your pride and fear. Launch out into the deep. Leave the comfort zone. Journey into the unknown and find a home for your heart. Rid yourself of loneliness—it is a narrow and demeaning state of mind.

Until you meet your soul mate and then start a family, or you find your niche professionally, give yourself wholly to you. Then, when the opportunity presents itself to enter into a meaningful relationship of any sort, you will be centered and capable of sustaining love.

Don't let bitterness bring you down.
Forgive and let live.

You are loved, esteemed, and accepted.

Go where you are celebrated
instead of tolerated.

THREE

Abandoned Heart

As a child, Bill Wilson was abandoned by his mother to fend for himself on the streets of Brooklyn. So deep was his sense of abandonment that today Bill rescues and ministers to street children. In them Bill sees himself and his horrific life story.

Amazingly, what was meant for evil, Bill turned around for good. Such a state of mind and an ability to harness one's emotions despite the terrible circumstances that contributed to them is nothing short of miraculous. Like Bill, we too can rise above our circumstances.

Abandonment comes in many sizes—yet it all hurts just the same. The reverse side of the coin of abandonment is trust. When an intense level of trust has been placed in a person, only to later be violated and broken, we are left feeling betrayed and abandoned. Such a feeling is like the wind being taken out of our sail, draining us of our energy and momentum. A blow to our self-confidence occurs as we begin to wonder why we were not worthy of appropriate affection and attention.

What we must remember however is the covenant breaker who abandoned us did so because of their own personal inadequacies and character flaws, not because of something we did necessarily. We must therefore forgive and release them. For in so doing we are releasing and freeing ourselves.

Holding on to feelings of abandonment engenders a deep-seated bitterness that does not serve us well. We are better off to forgive and let live, considering the loss to be the loss of the individual who left us. Abandonment leads to feelings of rejection, which are valid and very real. The way to rise above such feelings is to validate yourself, acknowledge your worth and personal value. Make a fresh commitment to yourself and affirm your personhood.

Regardless of what others say or do, you commit to love you. Remember, you were created in the image and likeness of God. The Creator of the universe loves you unconditionally, despite your mistakes and frailties. You therefore have a duty to honor the spark of eternity, the nature of God, within you. Lift your head up high and remember who you are!

Know assuredly that what one rejects, another gladly and joyfully accepts. There is no scarcity on this planet. There will most definitely be someone, if not many, who will celebrate your uniqueness and wholeheartedly embrace you as you are. You therefore must position yourself inwardly and outwardly to do the same without doubting.

Write some empowering rules to overcome the feeling of abandonment:

1. There are kind, compassionate people who want to lend a helping hand to assist me. I am never abandoned. I need to journey to the right people.

2. Abandonment is a temporary feeling in which God has given me a gift to look up to Him instead of out to humanity. I receive abandonment as an opportunity to connect with God and give place to my Creator to supernaturally intervene in my situation and be glorified.

You are loved, esteemed, and accepted. You may not have discovered yet who it is who loves and accepts you, but assuredly you were prepared for a person. Don't despise your uniqueness, nor belittle divine design. This is your time to shine!

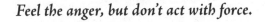

Feel the anger, but don't act with force.

We wrestle not against flesh and blood, but mindsets and spiritual wickedness.

Presumption opens up the door to much misunderstanding.

Ignoring your feelings does not do away with them.

Denying your tension only serves to make it boil all the hotter.

Validate your feelings, but maintain control.

Transformation comes when we deal with the roots rather than try to cut off the bad fruit.

FOUR

Angry Heart

SOME WOMEN, WHEN in abusive relationships, have sought to even the score with their husbands. For example, there was the story of Clara Harris, a Texas dentist who got twenty years in prison for killing her husband by running him over—three times. In another case, Jean Harris shot her boyfriend, Scarsdale Diet doctor Herman Tarnower.

As for men, celebrity divorce lawyer Raoul Felder says, "Men are challenged more by women at work and at home, and they're losing it."[1] Felder, the co-author of *Getting Away with Murder*, a 1996 study of domestic violence, says, "Most murders take place in the kitchen, and the second-most take place in the bedroom. It gives you some ideas of the priorities in this country."[2]

I once heard a famous pastor say that when he has to counsel couples dealing with domestic violence the first thing he wants to do is meet with the husband. Once alone with the man, he asks him about himself. It has been his experience that if the man has any degree of rage, it usually has to do with the man's poor self-image.

It is reasonably common that when we are down on ourselves is when we are most volatile toward others. Belligerent behavior is often preceded by negative internal dialogue with which we beat ourselves down. Then, when faced with outside pressures and people, we explode on whomever is closest. Sadly that is often the innocent spouse.

A feeling of powerlessness often precedes an episode of abuse. A continual nagging within one's conscience, accompanied by a lack

17

of self-confidence, can cause a person to snap and resort to violence as a means to feeling a sense of significance. As insane as it sounds, unfortunately it is true. We all seek to be empowered in some way. This however is the most depraved and perverted method to self-empowerment. This fleeting sense of power gained during abuse is the signal that someone has lost all self-control. Yet the harm done is irreparable. As for the man's seemingly empowering violent behavior, it is briefly attainable but not sustainable.

FEEL IT BUT DON'T ACT WITH FORCE

Anger is another wonderful emotion worthy of validation and acceptance. What we do with our anger however is important and needs to be scrutinized.

Anger often arises when we feel we have been disrespected, dishonored, or belittled. The problem appears when you are angry as the result of having misread someone and their intentions toward you. This is presumption and is quite common. Many of us often stereotype people. Then when they talk or act a certain way, we immediately group them within a particular classification, thinking ourselves to be wise enough to predict their motives and corresponding action. Such is not always the case however as we often misjudge and misread people.

Presumption opens the door to misunderstanding. When we try to read people and size them up, we diminish their person and potential.

Righteous anger is justifiable in the face of injustice. It is paramount that you stand up for yourself and those unable to defend themselves. Yet while doing so, you don't want to behave badly and ruin your good name. The Bible says, "Be angry and do not sin" (Eph. 4:26). Anger in itself is not a sin. It is what we do with it that can lead to sin.

We all lose our temper at times. Acknowledging the feeling of anger actually helps alleviate the emotional explosions that occur when we bottle up our feelings. Not acknowledging feelings and emotions does not do away with them. They are still there. Ignoring your inner tension only serves to make it boil all the hotter and eventually you lose it.

Recognize when you are angry. Reason with yourself in regard to why it is advantageous for you to calm down and get a grip on yourself. Maintaining inner control is much more effective than trying to get a grip on yourself outwardly. It is not good to project outwardly that you have it all together when inwardly you are steaming.

Some empowering rules I have written for myself in regard to anger are as follows:

1. Anger is a gift from God enabling me to discover what I am passionate about.

2. Anger is exciting because it moves me emotionally and enables me to channel my emotions productively rather than without control.

3. Anger is a wake-up call for me to practice self-control, to not be ruled by the external world, and be self-governing.

4. Anger resulting from frustration is an opportunity for me to think wisely and creatively on how I can achieve my goals differently than my current course of action.

We all lose it at times and succumb to feelings of anger. What is empowering however is to dig deeper and discover the frustration that led to your feelings of disappointment. Transformation comes when we deal with the roots rather than try to cut off the bad fruit.

---

1. Kevin Gray, *Details* magazine, Dec. 2004, 94–98.
2. Barbara Victor and Raoul Felder, *Getting Away With Murder: Weapons for the War Against Domestic Violence* (Carmichael, CA: Touchstone, 1999).

Make a decision, even if it is the wrong one.
You can always adjust, correct, and fix it
if it is wrong.

Confused people are present in body
but absent in mind.

Your sense of certainty is vital
for your mental health.

Bury confusion by being bold and
courageous and making a decision.

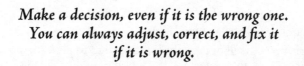

FIVE

Confused Heart

*I*DON'T KNOW WHAT to do?" How many times has a woman agonized over dating or dropping a guy? How often have you so scrutinized a relationship looking into the other's motives to the extent of only ending up more confused yourself?

The ways in which we drive ourselves into confusion are countless. A confused heart hindered by uncertainty is limited and incapacitated. You can often see it in people's eyes that they are not fully present—present in body but absent in mind. Plastic smiles adorn their faces while they are perplexed and dying inside.

Many people are not skilled at articulating their feelings. Merely distinguishing between "good" and "bad" emotions is not very helpful as it provides no useful information about what is going on to make you feel that way, or what to do to change your situation. On the other hand, knowing precisely which emotion you are feeling provides you immediately with useful feedback.

A high school principal asked for help because she felt "bad." When asked "What kind of bad?" she could only answer, "You know, just bad." "Bad" is simply a name for a class of generally unpleasant emotions. After some examples of the differences between feeling bad and feeling worried or scared or inadequate, she realized that the bad feeling she was experiencing was anxiety.

Once she knew that what she was feeling was anxiety, she was able to determine that her attention was focused on a future

21

filled with unknowns. She felt ill prepared to face some task or situation that held the possibility of unpleasant consequences, such as an upcoming confrontation with the school board. When the principal prepared to respond resourcefully, her anxiety was replaced with feelings of self-assurance and confidence.

Allow my poem to provide an illustration for you:

PERCEPTION

Perception is a compilation
Of your history
Through which you see
Erroneously or correctly
Your present reality
Perception affects your identity
Positively or negatively
Based on what you think
People believe you to be
Perception leads to projection
The good, bad, and ugly
As that which is within
Comes forth in expression
Whether it be embracing love
Or walls of rejection
Before you can proceed
Your inner self first must precede
To frame its image
And settle within
To be transparent and befriend
Or be reclusive and center in
To unconditionally accept humanity
Or prejudge and condemn individuality
Projection evolves into conception
Where thoughts, words, and actions give birth
To what you've already contextualized within
Resulting in an outward manifestation
An invitation to all of creation

To coexist with you
Help make your dream come true
Or confirm your nightmare too
To walk along with you
From conception to maturation
From coincidence to confirmation
From self-awareness to personal revelation
To give you a sneak preview
Of what your perception can do
How it can brighten or cloud you
Right or wrong
You carry it all day long
Projecting it in word and song
Continually conceiving from night to dawn
Not knowing why people respond
Some distant, others fond
Of you the perceiving one
Whose world within and without
Have come and gone
Sometimes in the company of friends
Other times with nobody to lean on
So judge nothing before the time
Though there be no reason or rhyme
For God is sublime
Knowing man must first discover himself
Before he can find
The presumptuous perception
That misleads him much of the time
A prison or paradise
You can have through perception
It's all up to you
Your illumination
Your imagination
Your stimulation
Your inner sensation
If it's going to be
It's up to me!

As a man thinks in his heart
So he is
This is no pop quiz
Come out therefore
From behind the bars
Take rest in paradise
And reach for the stars!

CAUSES OF CONFUSION

There is often a difference between what you observe about another person's behavior outwardly and what the person is actually feeling internally. Because people who are blind to their emotions have no way of understanding their blindness, their use of language can often be misleading and prevent others from detecting the problem.

Color blindness frequently goes undetected because one cannot miss something one has never experienced. There can be a similar scenario in the emotional realm, until one has been awakened to new emotions. It is one thing to use terms logically in language that you have never experienced and quite another to use the same terms when you have experienced such feelings and emotions.

Others who experience and know intuitively what they feel but find themselves unable to articulate it could be limited in their vocabulary. Perhaps they are just unwilling to face the emotional reaction that would occur from outsiders were they to be honest as to their feelings. Then there are some who condition themselves to conform to the way society tells us we should be and thus they are in an emotional straightjacket primarily because of fear of rejection.

Confusion can be caused by indecision within or without. External sources of confusion are primarily people who you have allowed to influence your life. Your sense of certainty is vital for your mental health. If other people are the source of your confusion because you are trying to read them and not sure, it is best to deliberately and boldly ask them where they stand. If they are unsure, you need to make a conscious decision where you stand. There is a time to wait for additional information and situations to become clearer. However once that time has come, you must make a decision and move on. Some things you do not need to know and others you may never know.

Liberating and empowering rules to overcome confusion can be:

1. Confusion is a feeling I honor and validate because it is a signal to me that I am not getting the results I desire. This feeling actually helps me save time and effort, rather than stubbornly and fruitlessly continue in the same course of action.

2. Confusion is an indicator that I have to go back to the drawing board and devise a new strategy of meeting my needs and obtaining my goals. Sometimes that means only a slight revision, correction, or adjustment after which I shall get tremendous and rapid results.

3. Confusion is my friend enabling me to fully think things through before spinning my wheels and being left unfulfilled due to improper planning.

4. Confusion is a gift that compels me to find people smarter than myself whom I can learn from and come into meaningful relationship with.

Refuse to stay in a state of confusion. Instead, let confusion lead you to discover deeper truths that will catapult you into the future for which you were created. Bury confusion by being bold and courageous and making a decision.

*Breathe deeply and keep your head up
where God intended it to be.*

*Create an atmosphere conducive to your
personal passion and pursuits.*

*Where your focus goes, feelings and energy
flows. Redirect your focus.*

Don't live in the "I should…" world.

Frame your world with your words.

*Detach yourself from your limiting beliefs
by objectively examining them
and replacing them with truth.*

*Do something extraordinary to free
yourself from the mundane!*

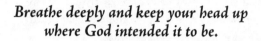

Six

Heavy Heart

A HOT AIR BALLOON cannot get off the ground until some of its weight is dropped and the encumbrances holding it back from ascending are cut. How about you? Are you ready to go higher in your life or are you happy to be entangled and tied down emotionally? How long will you tolerate attending your own pity party and coddle yourself emotionally?

Heaviness of heart can come from numerous influences you have allowed into your life. Remember, it is not about what is going on *around* you as much as *inside* of you. You must learn to control your own mental and emotional states. How do you do that? It is done by regulating your internal dialogue, focus, and physiology.

The way you carry your body and posture physically has a great deal to do with your emotional state and personal well-being. It begins with your breathing. Breathe deeply from your diaphragm and keep your head up where God intended it to be. Put your shoulders back and walk with confidence. Watch the immediate change that occurs inside of you as you do.

GET MOVING!

Incorporate cardiovascular exercise into your daily routine to ensure the greatest health benefits. Rigorous morning exercise speeds up your metabolic rate and gives you increased energy throughout the day. Exercising before breakfast always helps you burn more fat cells stored in your body.

If you find the gym to be boring, buy a trampoline and use it at home. Play tennis or racquetball. Kick a soccer ball. Shoot hoops. Do something. Get moving—motion precedes emotion. Go to the beach. Get a massage. Go fishing. Do something you enjoy. Take up a hobby. Join a dance class. Enlarge your social sphere. Push past your personal limits and break the spirit of heaviness off of your life.

People who have a hard time getting out of bed in the morning to go to a job they hate, who find it difficult to become engaged in their professional activities, and who feel emotionally dead after a day at the office, need to pay attention to those feelings. They are important signals that there must be another way to get more fulfillment out of life.

If such feelings of lethargy, passivity, and disinterest wear you down each day, then consider a change in occupation or a change in scenery or work environment. Modify the variables in your work life until you come to a place of personal joy, fulfillment, and ecstasy.

Guard your inner life and don't tolerate negative internal dialogue that throws you into a state of hopelessness and despair. Some people live in the world of "I should." A better, more assertive statement to get leverage on and maximum commitment out of yourself is "I will" or "I must." This is not an empowering emotional state by any means. Get a sense of certainty and self-confidence with which to take immediate action.

Look back in your life to a time when you were on top of the world, living at your optimum emotional state, high as a kite, exuding self-confidence and certainty. Now feel it! Relive and experience it afresh. Now anchor that feeling within you right now and own it again. See yourself at that emotional level in the now with what you are currently focusing on and engaged in.

The quickest way for me to break out of heaviness of heart is to turn on some fiery music that fills the atmosphere with passion. I then enter into that passion and possess it for personal use to peak my performance.

28

Learn how to create an atmosphere conducive to your personal pursuits and passions. Rid yourself of any other attitude or atmosphere that does not serve your inner awareness and personal goals. Replace every attitude and atmosphere with one of your own creation.

If you are at work and unable to change the atmosphere, create one within you wherever you are. Harness that energy from within and regulate your state rather than succumbing to and coming under the atmosphere generated by someone else that does not serve you.

God Himself has stated in His Word the necessity for us to "break forth into joy!" (Isa. 52:9). Before we can enter a joyful state, often we must first break out of the negative emotional state holding us captive. Get aggressive and grab hold of yourself. The moment you realize that you have fallen under heaviness and become entangled by an emotional octopus, do something immediately to break out and cut the tentacles!

FOCUS AND LANGUAGE

Your inner focus also should be positive, uplifting, encouraging, and progressive. What you focus on you feel. Where focus goes, energy flows. Why is that? Because what you behold and focus on you move toward. It is therefore paramount that you focus on the future that you intend to move toward.

Lastly, we must look at your language and the meaning you give it. Your talk must match where you want to walk in life. Words are containers, carrying you to your desired destiny. They direct you toward fulfilling that which you speak.

Write down your most limiting and destructive beliefs as you have habitually spoken them to yourself. Some people believe they cannot make it in life because they don't have an education. Others believe they aren't physically attractive. Another limiting belief is you don't have enough money. Whatever it is, detach yourself from it and objectively examine it for what it is.

29

Now rewrite your life story by stating the truth about yourself: "The truth is that, intuitively, I am wise and knowledgeable. So with or without an education I am well able to succeed in life because I am self-taught and a hands-on learner with tremendous people skills."

Let your new life story be shot forth like an arrow from a bow. Declare it with fiery passion, letting it purify your soul and renew your mind as you do.

"The truth is I have all the resources I need to be successful beginning with my wisdom, relationships, and reputation. I attract wealth to me as I'm a money magnet with whom others want to be associated." Write out as many rules as necessary to reinforce your personal value, purpose, and passions.

Some rules to liberate and uplift you concerning heaviness of heart are as follows:

1. Heaviness of heart is a gift because it points out to me that I have put unrealistic expectations on people, mere mortals who are prone to occasionally fail by reason of their flaws and faults.

2. Heaviness of heart is an indicator that I am focusing too much on myself and my needs rather than others and their needs.

3. Heaviness of heart is not a time to pity, but rather a time to throw a party and celebrate my family and friends whom I love.

4. Heaviness of heart is a temporary blessing showing me how others feel in the earth who are emotionally in need of me.

5. Heaviness of heart is a challenge from my Creator to lift up my eyes to the heavens where my help comes from. As I connect with God and His glory spills out over me, my countenance will shine again!

Help yourself by engaging in exhilarating activities physically, mentally, and spiritually. Enlarge your social circle and see a new reality emerge for you!

Love is reckless—it is all about vulnerability, transparency, and trust.

God only lets you play hide and seek for so long.

Eventually the walls are going to come tumbling down. When they do, if you are still hiding behind them, they will crush you.

Truth penetrates every fortress of fear.

The fire of the Spirit melts the hardest of hearts.

Hardness of heart is a signal that you need to forgive and live.

SEVEN

Hard Heart

I COULDN'T BRING DOWN her walls with a jackhammer!" This is how I felt about a significant other who had withdrawn and began stonewalling me. If she just had the decency to communicate her feelings I could have easily let her go. Enduring the silence and unanswered questions was the hardest part, making it awfully hard to move on.

I should not have been surprised as the darling of my heart had previously told me that when she thought anyone was going to break up with her, she would do so first. I wondered how many times she pulled the ax out prematurely in her own fear and aborted a good thing. Certainly in my case as I had no intention of leaving her.

I suppose her departure was a blessing in disguise as she had much emotional baggage to process. Behind the callous citadel that she had erected there was no emotional transparency or human decency. Her silent withdrawal left me playing an awkward guessing game with myself. She did not know what she was feeling because she was looking for outsiders to please and tell her what to feel and do.

Some people are hard on the outside, hunkered down and buried beneath their emotional fortress, that no one can penetrate their rough exterior. They talk such a good game and portray such a sense of self-control that many believe them. The protective mechanism does however serve a purpose, as it feels safer than enduring the risk of being hurt again.

Love is reckless. It is all about vulnerability, transparency, and trust. Many do not find fearless love an easy venture to pursue again. Therefore they erect walls behind which to hide and protect their fragile heart.

HEALING BROKEN HEARTS

God heals the brokenhearted and enables them to leap over walls built by emotional scars. Your Creator only lets you play hide-and-seek for so long. Eventually, circumstantial pressure and the right relational interaction will bring down the walls behind which hard-hearted people hide. Truth penetrates every fortress of fear and hammers strongholds down to the ground.

When the fire of God's Spirit touches you the meltdown begins and your hardness of heart melts in the presence of the Lord. There have been times of intense frustration in my own life when I was bitterly angry with God. Suddenly, when I least expected it, the Spirit of the Lord came upon me and melted me down to mush. An hour later I found myself coming up off the floor with tears streaming down my cheeks, followed by the most intense and triumphant joy bursting forth from within my belly.

Did I fully understand what had happened? Not in the least. However I enjoyed the feeling and touch of God nonetheless. I was free from hard-heartedness and nothing else mattered. I will take a breakthrough however I can get it! That is far more enjoyable than being rigid trying to figure everything out mentally. Excessive analysis can lead to paralysis mentally, spiritually, and emotionally.

Rivers were made to swim in not study. Strip yourself of the outer garments of your falsely constructed identity and jump in the river of God's Spirit and have some fun! This is your day—make the most of it!

Here are some rules to empower you when you sense your heart beginning to harden:

1. Hardness of heart is an indicator that your emotional focus is out of balance with that which really matters in life.

2. Hardness of heart is a signal that you need to forgive and live. When I forgive, immediately my heart begins to melt and become soft again.

3. Hardness of heart reveals bitterness in your heart toward God and others, showing that you are disconnected. If you can breathe, you can believe. As you believe again, your soul will experience the wind of heaven, which will blow all the debris currently hindering you out of your soul and relationships.

4. I break out of hardness of heart by visiting those who are tender in heart.

5. When my heart becomes hard I read God's Word which is likened to a hammer, a mirror, and a fire—all able to reshape, reveal, and melt me within.

Do not settle for being hard-hearted. Let the Father of all glory melt your heart by the fire of His Spirit. Connect with God the Father in sweet fellowship and watch His fire, fervor, and favor come upon your life.

Running, retreating, and removing yourself
from people and situations is not necessarily
the outcome you ultimately desire.

Whatever you run from will only follow you.

Awaken to the inner issue from which
you are running.

Denial does not diminish
what is doing you in.

A quiet retreat alone is often the breeding
ground of newfound truth and self-discovery.

Locate your life's direction
and lock into it.

When you are sure of the way to go
you won't stray every which way.

Eight

Wayward Heart

I'M GOING TO run away!" How many of us have said or heard that? How many of us have done it? How many of us have run away only to find ourselves shortly thereafter retreating and returning home realizing it wasn't so bad there after all?

Often, we do not physically run away, but internally we withdraw from a person or situation—only to find months, if not years, later we improperly assessed the situation. That is the result of hastily drawing conclusions about people and things you may not fully understand. Presumption or assumption is the great transgression. (See Psalm 19:12–13.) Assumption leads to professional and relational suicide.

Running, retreating, and removing yourself from people and situations is not necessarily the outcome you ultimately desire. Though doing so may bring temporary relief, inwardly you remain bound to run should similar types of people and circumstances show up in your life. Life on the run is not the most meaningful way to exist from day to day.

The movie *Runaway Bride* depicted a woman who was so double minded she didn't know which way was up. Once she got what she wanted, she no longer wanted what she had gotten. Isn't that how life is at times? Or perhaps we as humans evolve and change, as do our interests and desires. This makes commitment a bit complicated at times for the faint in heart.

Sometimes when we run we seemingly have to get hit upside the head with a two-by-four before we awake to the inner issue from which we are running. A wayward heart is often ignoring an inner issue that it is refusing to deal with and tackle head on. Such a person lies to himself and tries to disassociate from the pain. Not having time for the pain, they deny it and run from it altogether. The truth, however, is that when we live in denial and run from the pain we only perpetuate, deepen, and worsen it.

When you break your arm, you can ignore it all you want but that doesn't put it back into place. To ignore is to tend toward ignorance by reason of denial. Denial however does not diminish or deplete the thing that has disrupted your life. It is far better to deal with it than run from it.

When we run we only remove ourselves from our surroundings to get a clearer picture of who we are or are not. It is often here that our illusion of who we thought we were is shattered and the real you is discovered. Why is it we get so enamored with our circumstances that we let them get entrenched within us and lose our own identity?

Under such pressures we need to run away—from things only, not people. A quiet retreat by yourself is often the breeding ground for newfound truth and self-discovery. Personal awareness is often quite low with people as they are often too engrossed critiquing everyone else to take a good hard look at themselves.

Rules to conquer a wayward heart and get back on track:

1. Waywardness of heart when revealed to me is an opportunity to humble myself, admit my wrongs and the instances I have erred in my decisions. When I humble myself and acknowledge my missteps, mercy and grace flow to me and reposition me where I need to be.

2. When I feel wayward, like the black sheep in the family, it is an opportunity for me to come to a greater level of self-awareness, embrace personal discovery, and celebrate my own uniqueness.

3. Feelings of waywardness are illuminating when I detach myself (my identity) from the emotion and carefully observe it. Through careful observation I can discover whether I am experiencing this emotion due to an inclination for conformity and compliance or rebellion and rejection.

4. The emotional pull and realization of waywardness is a gift enabling me to become honest with myself and more deeply establish my sense of certainty and life's direction.

Seek to discover your life's direction and pinpoint your purpose. Waywardness of heart is often the result of not having locked into a higher goal or deeper desire worth living for. Locate your life's direction and lock into it.

*Trust requires that I be vulnerable
and transparent with people.*

*Do not emotionally hold people hostage
because of your personal unfinished business.*

If you get ditched, you get discernment.

If you get burned, you get better.

If you get broken, you can get a breakthrough.

*To not be vulnerable, relatable, and real
is to risk never connecting on a deep level
with people.*

*Connect with people and don't fear
those who reject.*

*When people remove themselves
from you, consider it their loss.*

*Don't let distrust cause you to reject
meaningful relationships.*

NINE

Distrusting Heart

MARRIAGE IS NOT always an easy alliance. Infidelity strikes at the core of our being and personal dignity. Distrust therefore can be a battle we have to deal with before we wear ourselves out emotionally and begin to trust the person we are with or remove them from our lives altogether.

Historically, distrust has been a bug that eats at the human soul. Othello smothered Desdemona because he thought she cheated on him; Hercules killed his wife in a fit of madness (claiming the gods made him do it); and in *The Arabian Nights*, the Great Sultan, believing all women are wicked, married a fresh wife each night and had her strangled the following morning. Indeed there is nothing new under the sun as it pertains to human distrust in relationships. (See Ecclesiastes 1:9.)

Trust requires that we be vulnerable and transparent with people. That is more easily said than done because all of us fear rejection at some level. The key to hurdling that barrier is to decide in your heart that if you get burned, you get better. If you get ditched, you get more discernment. If you get hurt, God can heal your heart and help you up again! No guts, no glory!

Sadly, some who have been hurt take their pain into their new relationships and perpetuate and complicate their emotional lives holding their newfound love beneath their microscopic scrutiny until they prove out. That is they hold them guilty until proven innocent based upon the actions of others who have wronged them. It is far better however to start afresh and not hold people hostage emotionally because of your personal unfinished business. Forgive and let live!

To not be vulnerable, relatable, and real is to risk never connecting with people. It is far worse to be unable to connect with people than to connect with and be cut off by people. Connect and don't fear those who might reject you. When people remove themselves from you, consider it their loss. Consider it a blessing in disguise as God is getting ready to give you more meaningful relationships.

Refuse to allow distrust to impede your relational development and progress. Don't let distrust cause you to reject meaningful relationships. Trust and thrust yourself forth to new levels in your relationships.

Rules to rid yourself of distrust and its crippling effects:

1. I give everyone the benefit of the doubt and consider them innocent before guilty.

2. I have decided to err on the side of mercy and grace rather than judgment and criticism.

3. When I show hope and faith in humanity, people most often meet my expectations and bless my life.

4. Trust empowers people around me and makes them want to help me.

Don't be disabled by distrust. Whatsoever is not of faith is sin, but if you will break forth as a believer you will always win. Lift up your head! The sun always shines above the clouds. Don't let anybody rain on your parade. Keep the party pumping and celebrate you today!

Your decisions determine your feelings.

Channel your feelings by your focus.

*A broken heart, though painful, can lead to
a positive experience.*

*When it seems you are broken, God has
a way of breathing afresh upon your soul
and making you whole.*

*Our Maker is the Master at creating
a new beginning for His children.*

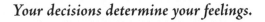

Ten

Broken Heart

"YOU BROKE MY china horses!" My mother lost her temper as she realized her prized collection had been broken during the move. After regrouping, she patiently glued the salvageable ones back together.

How patient are we with our own hearts when they get broken? Not nearly as patient it seems in a culture where we are always expected to "get it together." Perhaps it would serve us well in times of personal brokenness to be patient with ourselves while we recover. The repair process takes longer for some than others.

One man whose wife left him told me that he took two years off and did not date anyone. As for me, I gave my ex-wife two months to show herself committed to our marriage after confessing her infidelity. When she remained unrepentant, I divorced and moved on.

Upon divorcing, I moved on and joyfully put myself back into circulation. My decisions determine my feelings, emotion following my motion. My focus channels my feelings. My past does not determine my future.

Brokenness of heart, though painful, can be a positive experience. It is during these times of intense brokenness that we are most susceptible to God's touch and gentle voice. Faithful friends resurface in our times of emotional trauma. Fair-weather friends are revealed for who they are. Your life's foundation is revealed for you to see what it is made of.

When it seems you are shattered and broken, God has a way of breathing upon your soul and making you whole. A simple word from your Creator, such as "I love you!" can make you feel brand new in who you are as a person made in your Maker's image.

It is when you feel broken that God helps you get repositioned and readjusted in Him. He forms and fashions you into a new creation, forging for you a new destination. Our Maker is the Master at creating a new beginning for His children.

Remember the sun always shines above the clouds. Just look up to heaven where your help comes from. Lift up your heart to heaven. Look unto the Author and Finisher of your faith and live again.

Some empowering rules to apply when you feel broken are:

1. When my heart feels broken, I give thanks because I can feel my heart.

2. When feeling brokenhearted I fall into the arms of God, who is able to heal my heart.

3. When my heart is broken I honor the feelings but evaluate precisely what person and/or action led to this emotion. Upon doing so I gain insight and wisdom that makes me stronger, more self-aware, and ready for relationships.

4. To the extent I feel the depths of sorrow, I also will feel the depths of love, the heights of exhilarating joy, and fully appreciate them when they come my way. Such acceptance of the bad times makes for greater appreciation of the good times and the ability to maintain meaningful relationships.

Becoming hard-hearted only makes life harder. Live and let live. Have a hearty sense of self-esteem with which you can joyfully roll with whatever life brings you. When your heart takes a hit, bounce back with boundless love and triumphantly endure it. True love is not self-seeking. Therefore when you are emotionally bruised, get up off the ground and say "Next!" knowing that another special soul eagerly awaits the love you have got to give.

*Get up! Stand up for yourself! Fight for
your self-respect and personal dignity.*

*When all hell seems to be breaking loose,
truly all hell is breaking loose.*

*When feeling overwhelmed,
prepare to overcome.*

*You have all you need within you to organize
your life and overcome your challenges.*

God is for you—who can be against you?

*Forget the horrors of yesterday.
Today is yours for the taking.*

ELEVEN

Overwhelmed Heart

I CAN'T TAKE IT any more!" Screaming at the top of his lungs, falling to his knees, and looking upward, my new roommate seemed drastically overwhelmed to say the least. I had just moved from Florida to California to attend Bible school and the one person I was referred to for a possible living situation was rather interesting. Little did I know all of the complexities I was getting myself into. At the age of twenty-six he had a co-dependent relationship with mommy and an unwillingness to hold a job. Later I learned of a car accident he was in that left him with a massive head injury and his car totaled. His doctor had begun heavily medicating him and told him he would never work again.

I don't know what makes some doctors think they can offer a verdict along with their diagnosis. It only has the effect of removing hope from the human soul. Maybe God should send some physicians a lightning bolt to awake them to their position, lest they continue overstepping their bounds.

As for my roommate, I refused to be brought down his emotional slide by being overwhelmed with him. I tolerated no excuses, which made me appear quite heartless I'm sure. Regardless of what it felt like emotionally, I knew I was right and determined to hold to my position.

What you tolerate eventually dominates your life. Stand up for your rights—don't give up. My boldness and abrasive determination drove all of us from the comfort zone into the courageous danger zone. With guts and faith I really declared war on the home front.

Although his condition looked like a breakdown, it was actually the beginning of a glorious breakthrough. When all hell seems to be breaking loose, truly all hell is breaking loose! My roomy and I were soon of one mind and heart to cut the umbilical chord to his doctor's reports and his mother's worry. In the end, my roommate experienced a magnificent transformation. Today he owns his own computer company, drives a BMW, and is truly living the abundant life.

Now what about you? What areas of your life have you buried, stopped believing for, and allowed to die? Why have you stopped believing and living? What lies have you believed that are holding you back?

Let's write up some rules for coping with feelings of being overwhelmed:

1. No matter what unexpected things happen to me, I am never overwhelmed—just overcoming.

2. God is not punishing me. He is giving me a gift and challenging me to do what He already knows I am capable of.

3. I have all I need inside of me to organize my life and overcome my difficulties.

4. I will never say die or give in to outside influences when the greater One is in me, giving me the ability to be all that I desire to be!

You may be knocked down, but you are certainly not knocked out! Get up—go for it again! Harness your strength and go to battle. Your best days and blessed days are ahead of you. Leave the horrors of yesterday behind. Today is yours for the taking. Milk it for all it's worth!

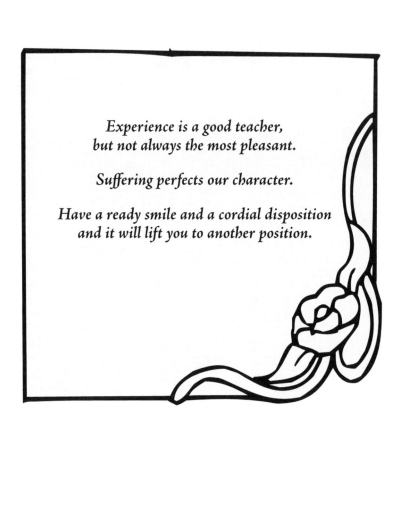

Experience is a good teacher,
but not always the most pleasant.

Suffering perfects our character.

Have a ready smile and a cordial disposition
and it will lift you to another position.

TWELVE

Tender Heart

"N̲ANA, I DON'T feel good." Sick and lying in bed, unable to play or go to school, I was demoralized. Thankfully my beloved grandmother came in to sit with me. As she rubbed my back and spoke reassuring words I felt a little better. Her acts of kindness—getting me juice and soup, checking on me periodically, and sitting with me—made the flu a bit more bearable.

How often do you show such unconditional love and tenderness to others? Who in your life has been tenderhearted and kind like that to you? What profound impact did it have on your heart and life?

Have you ever been heartless and withheld tenderness from someone in need? I know a particular incident when a young man came to me saying, "My girlfriend left me." I abruptly said to him, "Get over it."

Years later as I look back upon that situation, I realize I was totally clueless as to what he was going through. At that time I had never experienced such a thing. I therefore was not fit to comfort or advise anyone concerning such a situation. Years later however after having gone through a breakup and felt the depths of despair, I am well able to comfort and encourage such a person. Experience is a good teacher, but not always the most pleasant.

Life's circumstances serve to teach us life lessons and tenderize our hearts. This process makes for a kinder and more sympathetic person in each of us, capable of nurturing others and maintaining meaningful relationships. Perhaps this is why bad things happen to good people. By grand design, all of us suffer trials in order that we would be perfected in our character.

Here are some empowering rules for obtaining and sustaining a tender heart throughout life's ups and downs:

1. As a cook tenderizes meat with a hammer before cooking, so too life's experiences serve to soften my heart, making me more understanding and desirable relationally.

2. I don't seek to put my outlook on life on other people, but rather accept them by loving them unconditionally.

3. When I provide a sympathetic ear, tenderness flows through me.

As my Pop-Pop used to say, "It costs nothing to be nice." I have tried it and it truly does enhance your life. Have a ready smile and a cordial disposition and it will lift you to another position as you navigate through life—not to mention, people will take a shine to you and enjoy seeing you.

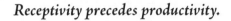

Receptivity precedes productivity.

It is amazing how much you can learn after you already know it all.

Your heart is the temple of God where communication is to occur.

Pleasure, possessions, power, and privilege are ultimately worthless in comparison to the indescribable joy of knowing God.

God gave you two ears and one mouth— listen twice as much as you speak.

Any dream worth pursuing is bigger than you. It will require outside input and assistance to see it come true.

Thirteen

Receptive Heart

WHAT NEW INFORMATION, insightful illuminations, or personal revelations have you come to that will enable you to grow? Have you blocked all outside stimuli thinking you already know it all? If so, how does that hinder your personal growth? What limitations are you installing by thinking you do not need to hear from anybody else in your life?

Receptivity precedes productivity. The first avenue of openness and receptivity is toward your Creator after which all other earthly relationships follow. The better connected you are vertically, the more relatable you are horizontally with humanity.

The time you take trying to be a know-it-all could be utilized elsewhere if you would have the humility to learn from someone who is already where you want to be. It is amazing how much you can learn after you already know it all.

Divine companionship is available for us all. It exists within the inner life, the secret place of continual abiding. Your heart is the temple of God. Communication with the Creator is not only to occur when difficulties are buffeting your life. Such cries in times of emergencies are urgent and indeed heard by God, but do not serve to build an inner stability and abiding relationship to bless you daily. In your Creator's presence is fullness of joy. God's presence makes you feel so loved, accepted, and wanted that your heart bubbles over with joy and your mind is as tranquil as calm waters. The Spirit of God is both mighty and gentle. When He comes upon you, every fiber of your being feels His power. And

His slightest touch can heal any sickness, break any bondage, vanquish any evil, and move any mountain.

God has made us to be carriers of His Holy Spirit. This wonderful, gentle, mighty Person within the Trinity wants to fill your life to overflowing. Pleasure, possessions, power, and privilege are ultimately worthless in comparison to the indescribable joy of knowing God.

Rivers of blessing flow as you begin to daily commune with your Creator within your heart. Internal awareness is established, emotional intelligence is developed, and acute sensitivity to life's opportunities break forth in you when you connect with your Creator. Keep an open heart to God. Divine life, light, love, peace, and joy flow to us naturally and spontaneously. As we commune with and directly receive from our Creator, we get a fresh impartation of eternal life.

Here are some empowering rules to maintain receptivity as a core value in your life to generate countless blessings and separate you from the norm:

1. Receptivity is a part of my disposition when I maintain an attitude of gratitude, heart of humility, and delightful expectation of humanity.

2. As I practice humility, my receptivity and productivity increases hundredfold.

3. Confrontation and criticism (though temporarily uncomfortable) are gifts and opportunities for me to reevaluate and make personal improvements for the better.

4. God gave me two ears and one mouth. When I listen twice as much as I speak, I benefit more.

Receptivity is an opportunity for you to receive and give to yourself through the input of others. As you hear your counselors and critics with an open heart, you will be more tuned into what matters most and the path you need to take to realize the fulfillment of your dreams.

Any dream worth pursuing is bigger than you, meaning it will require outside input and assistance to see it come true. Figure out early that you cannot make it alone in life and enjoy it wholeheartedly.

When we dare to discover and learn of God
we often come to a realization and
knowledge of ourselves.

Questioning the deeper meaning of life
can produce a great awakening.

As you connect with your Creator, expect
to be taken to a deeper place of revelation
and self-awareness.

Awakenings usually accompany significant
transitions in our personal and
professional lives.

A true awakening affects your vision,
purpose, and spirit.

It is when we lay down our
preconceived perceptions that our
biggest breakthroughs occur.

Fourteen

Awakened Heart

ARE YOU READY for a great awakening? Be assured that at some time in your life you will have a great awakening. Life has a way of testing our foundations, ideological beliefs, and the standards by which we live to see if they are pure and able to withstand the test of time. Everything that can be shaken will be shaken.

There are three types of knowledge:

1. The knowledge of others and things

2. The knowledge of God

3. The knowledge of self

Typically we master the first body of knowledge in part and leave the other two untouched. When we dare to discover and learn of God we often come to a knowledge of ourselves. Along this journey most of us only go so far as we prefer to lie to ourselves rather than fess up to the areas that need to be adjusted in our lives. Not to mention some areas of our lives that have been improperly built and need to be reconstructed properly so they can last and endure.

A GREAT AWAKENING

Questioning the deeper meaning of life can be very enlightening and produce a great awakening. Our minds are constantly active, always moving about, jumping here, there, and everywhere in thought. Tapping into the mind of God and getting beyond the mental fog of distractions that typically obscure the greater picture and grand design of our Creator can be challenging. The fog of distracting thoughts is very real, though not impenetrable.

Breaking through the mental barrier is a fight that cannot be won on your own. It is a spiritual battle. It is like trying to see across the street on a foggy day. Nothing you can do physically will help move that fog away. You have to simply be patient and wait for the fog to thin. Occasionally, a clear patch ahead emerges through which you can get a glimpse of what lies ahead. Our thoughts are just the same. Through inner solitude and a place of withdrawal for meaningful meditation, our thoughts can come from a deeper place and thereby be intertwined with the divine Spirit with which we all are connected.

The purpose of meditation is to stop thinking for a time, wait for the fog of thought to thin, and glimpse the spirit within. The Holy Spirit quickens and guides your spirit when you take time to quiet your soul and listen. (See John 6:63; Romans 8:16.)

A good place to begin meditation is on one thing that you can be fully fixated upon and is difficult to stray from in thought. As you connect with your Creator, expect to be taken to an even deeper place of revelation and self-awareness with which untold insights will emerge.

The great Albert Einstein said, "The true value of a human being is determined primarily by how he has attained liberation from the self."[1]

It is therefore up to us to free ourselves from our own self-imposed prison. As we enlarge our hearts, help from heaven and humanity moves toward us!

Awakening is a rousing from sleep, an emerging from a state of indifference, lethargy, or dormancy. It is when you become fully conscious, aware, and appreciative. As author of *From Coach to Awakener*, Robert Dilts says, "Times of growth and transformation in our lives are usually accompanied by such 'awakenings.' Consequently, awakenings usually accompany significant transitions in our personal and professional lives."[3]

We come out of our self-imposed stupor and the blindness is removed by the entrance of great illumination breaking forth from within. As we regain our internal sight and the eyes of our heart open, our world enlarges and brightens. Old perceptions and limitations which we previously succumbed to and slumped under are thrown off as we arise to live in a completely new way.

A great awakening brings about cognitive and mental expansion, affecting one's emotions and invigorating the heart within. As we reconnect with our motivations and stimulations at a deeper level and endeavor to go deeper, the dawn of day radiates forth from within the human soul.

A true awakening affects your vision, purpose, and spirit. It goes beyond the self-centered world. It involves your roles, values, beliefs, thoughts, actions, and sensations. It presses further to discover for whom and for what you were created. An awakening has a spiritual affect that reaches beyond self to apprehend and connect with family, community, the world, and the Creator. The motivation behind some of the greatest human achievements has been spiritual in the form of one's vision, life mission, and purpose. Many of the world's most important leaders and geniuses have acknowledged the significance of spiritual guidance in their lives and work.

Albert Einstein claimed:

> Science without religion is lame, religion without science is blind.[4]

When your mind connects to the Spirit, encompassing the collective universal whole, great enlightenment and profound discoveries can be the result. The social system and planetary ecology are all interconnected. God daily provides all of us with contexts and experiences that bring out the best in us as we seek to become more self-aware of our purpose, self, and the larger systems to which we belong.

It is a wonderful thing to step outside of the box. As a life coach it is my privilege and good fortune to be able to help people awaken to the deeper truths that they neglect to acknowledge. It is with skill and sensitivity that a greater level of self-awareness occurs. Such an awakening can either be gradual or sudden; sometimes it extends throughout different periods of one's life.

Life is a discovery process, even a mystery of sorts, with incredible possibilities for those who seek and dig deeper. Creating something completely new through the coach-client relationship is extraordinary and exciting. When people know that they are valuable and unconditionally accepted as they are, they will more readily perceive their other choices and make the right choices freely evolving in their intended direction.

It is OK to be you. People often limit the choices they perceive because they are still asleep to their authenticity. It is when we lay down our preconceived perceptions that our biggest breakthroughs occur.

Einstein's theory of relativity emerged because he asked himself questions about space and time without any preconceptions—the way a child would wonder about it. Possessing a childlike heart and playfulness about learning enables us to expand our minds and enlarge our creative awareness. It is a powerful gateway to facilitate an awakening. Here are some empowering rules to awaken you and bring about awakenings all around you:

1. I can awaken my heart by changing location geographically, people relationally and my mindset internally.

2. The unexpected and uncomfortable awakens my heart as I resolve the next course of action.

3. I choose to awaken daily to new sights, sounds, stimuli, and experiences by being playful and innocent.

4. I embrace divine interruptions in my life knowing that they often serve to bring about a great awakening in me.

Great awakenings do not come without a cost. Often that cost is your time, blood, sweat, and tears. Ironically, when you are being set up by divine design for a great awakening, you are often unaware of it and oppose the initial pain of the process. Then suddenly, the light bulb comes on and you are brought to a new understanding that propels you into your greater purpose.

1. Alice Calaprice, *The Quotable Einstein* (Princeton, NJ: The Hebrew University of Jerusalem and Princeton University Press, 1996), 89.
2. Robert Dilts, *From Coach to Awakener* (Capitola, CA: Meta Publications, 2003) 239.
3. Ibid.
4. Alice Calaprice, *The Quotable Einstein*.

God gave us a backbone for a reason. Let us not cower but courageously arise to conquer!

What would you die for? What pulls at your heartstrings? What injustice infuriates you and compels you to action?
Herein is found your purpose.

Go forth wholeheartedly with unstoppable intensity.

Do what you love and let the blessings follow.

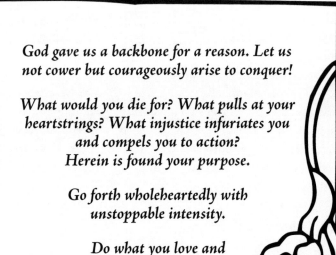

Fifteen

Brave Heart

WHEN OUR NATION was attacked by terrorists on 9–11, I could not find anyone to go to New York with me from my home state of Florida. The airports were all shut down for security reasons and the only means of getting there was by car. At the last minute a courageous young man joined me to make the trip. Upon our arrival we found ourselves at Ground Zero working with the Salvation Army.

It was a great honor to serve our country in its darkest hour. Yet that would never have happened had we not taken a leap of faith and boldly defied the odds. Indeed that historic moment at Ground Zero with the President, the New York Police Department, the fire fighters, and rescue workers was the greatest patriotic moment of my life.

How many of us take bold acts of courage when faced with a crisis personally, within our family, among our community, or even at a national level? This is what bravery is made of. God gave us a backbone for a reason. Let us not cower but courageously arise to conquer. We must remember that if what we are living for is not worth dying for, then it is not worthy of our life. Most live for mere survival. Others have broken out to personal enjoyment and accumulation of this world's goods. Yet how many of us live for a cause or a purpose we are passionate about?

FREEDOM OF EXPRESSION

I had the good fortune of listening to Anita Roddic, the founder of The Body Shop, talk about how she founded her company. What I find most impressive is Anita's inner motivations that are the force behind what she does. Anita recently told an assembly at the International Coach Federation, "Don't seek to make money. Seek freedom."[1]

Freedom was the motivating factor that propelled this entrepreneur to accomplish great things. Anita sought freedom of expression first, to express her ideological and social beliefs that she passionately cares about. Anita's Body Shop was the business that provided a platform to do so. As an agent for social change, Roddic has used the business she founded to serve the public's greater good first and foremost.

Who are you serving? What cause are you fighting for? I am poised to fight a battle for the brokenhearted. I am now able to tear down the walls of heartache and set the captives free. Equipped for and skilled in battle, I am stronger and wiser. My skin is now thicker, my heart stronger, my mind wiser, and my discernment sharper. What was meant for evil has been turned around for good. My emotional misery has been made into ministry for the masses. My hurt has prepared me to heal the multitudes. My brokenness has positioned me for personal breakthrough, which I can now accomplish for you. Like a wrecking ball, with a vengeance I can demolish the destructive enemies of your soul.

Is there anything that you would die for? What pulls at your heartstrings? What injustice infuriates you and compels you to action? What do you love and hate? What are you most passionate about? What could you not live without?

Here are some rules to live by to cultivate bravery and spontaneity of action:

1. I am brave when I feel fear but press on anyway.

2. I am brave when I hear what the naysayers are saying but do what I know to be true.

3. I am brave when I walk by faith, not by sight.

4. I am bold and courageous when I am led by what God has said concerning my life.

Commit to a cause. Be bold and take action. Nothing happens until you hunker down and dare to do. Don't bend, break, or bow. Arise to be everything our Creator intended you to be.

Boldness has genius, creativity, and magnetism. Do what you love and let the blessings follow you. Go forth wholeheartedly with unstoppable intensity.

---

1. Speech at International Coach Federation in Quebec, Canada,

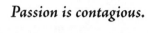

Passion is contagious.

Live a bold, authentic life.

God gave you one life—live it like there is no tomorrow.

Live so you have no regrets.

Let passion be your fuel.

Leave doubt in the dust and pursue your dreams with dogged determination.

Sixteen

Passionate Heart

A HEART ABLAZE. THAT was what American gymnast Kerri Strug had when she pressed through her injury to earn a gold medal for her performance in the 1996 Olympic games.

People are attracted to pursuing their passions and surrounding themselves with passionate people. Passion is contagious and invigorating. When asked what passion is, one person said, "I don't know what it is, but I know what it's not." Certainly passion can be felt and arouses the emotions. Many people have lost the art of living with passion and have taken the safe road of living cautiously.

Kids do not live like that. Children don't concern themselves with injuries and living delicately. They dive into activities and sports wholeheartedly, throwing caution to the wind. Somehow along life's journey we calm down, de-intensify, and settle into conformity.

God blesses each of us with one life. We are to live it like there is no tomorrow! Live so you have no regrets at the end of this grand journey. Pursue your dreams with a vengeance. If you are going to fail, fail at something you enjoy doing! If you don't take chances, you don't make advances!

How many of us do things we don't enjoy doing to survive? It does not have to be that way. If you would be bold and give yourself fully to your passion, you would see a way for you to fulfill your dreams. Jesus said: "According to your faith let it be to you" (Matt. 9:29). Sadly, many people have more negative faith than they have faith to arise and conquer their present reality. This is

71

not to say there are not small steps that one must take en route to designing a glorious future. Such sacrifices must also often be made. However passion must be the fuel driving you the whole way through.

To outwardly perform, you must first be inwardly driven with unstoppable zeal and determination. It takes a great deal of frustration and personal pain to push some beyond their comfort zone. In the interest of not wasting any more time, why not just see yourself ten years from now, having made no progress, and feel that excruciating disappointment for a while. If that doesn't feel good, take that feeling and harness it as motivation to catapult you to get started.

Pray with passion. Live with passion. Work with passion. Thrust forth into a new beginning with unstoppable determination. Let passion work for you and carry you to unlimited personal growth and satisfaction.

Here are some rules to generate passion in you to propel you to the next level in your life:

1. I am passionate when I am pursuing my dreams and not focusing on my limitations.

2. I am passionate when I am intensely present in spirit, soul, and body.

3. I am passionate within, despite my surroundings on the outside.

4. I am passionate when I live my dreams wholeheartedly.

5. My passion is unstoppable. Even when I rest, my passion burns hot as I envision my future and allow destiny to carry me to it.

I set my intent and don't let what I do not know prevent my forward progress en route to the desired destination. The people

I allow into my life are either fueling my passion or being energized by my passion. I do not allow or tolerate drainers of my passion. You were born an original. Don't die a copy. Write your life story with originality.

The rock group Bon Jovi wrote a great song called "It's My Life" that captures the heart of a passionate overcomer.

You're not going to live forever. Get up then and boldly live your dreams while you're alive!

Love fearlessly, believe continually, and boldly dare to do the impossible! Let your passion propel your life!

Prayer for Passion, Potency, and Unlimited Possibilities

Pray this prayer out loud as a vocal proclamation and divine invitation for supernatural breakthroughs to occur in and through your life.

> *Heavenly Father, thank You for sending Your Son Jesus to earth to model life without limits and love without walls. As Jesus passionately endured the cross for the sins of humanity and broke the barriers of death, Father, help me to live in newness of life in Christ.*
>
> *Thank you, Jesus, for dying for me and loving me unconditionally. Please forgive me of my sins—things done and left undone in my life. Wonderful Jesus, please come into my heart by the power of the Holy Spirit by which you rose from the dead and cause me to know the power of the resurrection with which I can live abundantly, love fearlessly, believe continually, progress passionately, and leave a legacy before I see You in eternity.*

About the Author

Discover Your Destiny, Build Your Dreams & Break Your Limitations!

Co-create a compelling future to live for with Paul as your personal Life Coach. Paul is a member of the International Coach Federation, a Master NLP Practitioner, a mediator trained in Conflict Resolution & Peacemaking, and a certified Personal Fitness Trainer. Whatever your need or goal, Paul is well equipped to empower you—spirit, mind, and body—to experience relational and professional fulfillment.

To book Paul to speak at your event, conference,
or seminar write or call
RevivingNations@yahoo.com ◆ (407) 967-7553
For additional information visit
www.DreamMakerMinistries.com
www.CreativeCommunications.TV

Other books by Paul Davis include *Do's and Don'ts Before You Say "I Do", Are You Ready for True Love?, Dream Voyage,* and *Destiny Discovery.* See the above Web sites for a full listing of all books, videos, and products.